The November Optimist

D1194441

The November Optimist

David Zieroth

*

GASPEREAU PRESS LIMITED
PRINTERS & PUBLISHERS
MMXIII

Who are we, who is each of us, if not a combinatoria of experiences, information, books we have read, things imagined?

FROM 'SIX MEMOS FOR THE NEXT MILLENNIUM' BY ITALO CALVINO, TRANSLATED BY PATRICK CREAGH

But you have a beautiful face, such a pleasant and— as I would like to add—interesting appearance, present such a fine aspect, look so candidly, majestically, calmly out of your eyes upon me as upon the world in general, that I could not possibly have compelled myself to pass you by without daring to say something or other flattering to you, which I hope you will not hold against me, although I am afraid that I deserve, if not correction, at least admonition on account of my frivolity.

FROM 'THE WALK' BY ROBERT WALSER, TRANSLATED BY CHRISTOPHER MIDDLETON WITH SUSAN BERNOFSKY

S o how would i describe you? Would I place you among your weekend women friends around Beans' indestructible tables, holding a latte and half-staring past the conversation toward a special chair back home where you curl and reflect and file and delete the day's events as naturally as brushing your long hair?

Or would you settle in one of the fat chairs in front of the fake fireplace, a large wall of light pouring onto your right shoulder, a magazine as a shield against that man with the grey ponytail—not me!—who fills the chair kitty-corner and who keeps looking/not-looking your way? You could tell he's about to comment, holding up a cardboard sign upon which he has written in square black letters: Would you like to talk—i.e., listen? What will you say when he eventually speaks, about the fireplace, the magazine, the light (probably not the light), your lemon green socks (probably not your socks, probably he knows personal comments will be rebuffed—surely he knows)? It's not what he says, but how you respond. A smile, cold and clear? A tossed-off phrase, 'yeah' or 'hmm'? Or will you simply ignore him, pretend you don't hear, toss *Cuisine Today* onto the table and walk your lemon green socks away?

On your way out, you notice one young man reading a paperback. Short, very black hair like a mat but one that is already trained to attend to his mirror-whims, finely intent eyes behind black-rimmed glasses (eyes

8   that glimmer and reel with opinions of literature), his
    forehead a smooth slab of white marble, in front of his
    face he holds up his black-rimmed Penguin classic, a
    totem, to blank out the hubbub around him even more
    effectively than his slow raising of the muffin and jam
    to his straight lips. A literature student, a grad student
    (though he doesn't have the sweetness of verisimilitude
    driven out of him yet: you can tell he still loves the thing
    as much as the theory of the thing), or perhaps that most
    surprising of beings, a genuine, eclectic reader. You bend
    down to catch the title, and you're tempted to say 'I've
    never seen anyone reading *him* here before,' but you know
    you would only distract our young man, turn his pleasure
    into embarrassment that someone would comment so
    baldly, here in public where he has come to escape his
    sweaty roommates and their whining about work shifts
    and essays, so he could be alone among denizens of the
    caffeine jungle and relish more deeply the horror (I've
    looked up my own copy and found this):

> *Let a man so much as scrape his finger pushing a truck in the
> pickle rooms, and he might have a sore that would put him out of
> the world; all the joints in his fingers might be eaten by the acid,
> one by one.*

As you step past, you see how delicately he picks up his
cup, half-self-consciously flexing his trembling pinkie
as he nibbles his muffin, still sure that before him lies
no such vile future. You feel so fond of him, he could be

your son, son of a woman with lemon green socks, she 9
who reads and wants to talk to those strangers who read
conjured worlds no longer here on earth.

Can I describe you at all? Have I said anything? Can
you be this almond fragrance, curve of ash blonde hair (or
is that light grey?), glance like a motion-activated lawn
light, mouth of pleasure and half-revealed anxiety, but no
defeat where lips meet, and the angle of your head and the
hint in your eyes agree that inner chores are not always
managed well when work and worry grow and gain, and
the future presses with its inescapably still-yearning
inscape? And will I ever be able to know you so well that I
might say you're

> *Sometimes untidy, often elegant,*
> *So easily hurt, so readily responsive …*
> *Whose fingers curl and melt*
> *When you are friendly …?*

A CRIB MATTRESS FLIPS OFF a moving van hurtling up
the slope of the Second Narrows Bridge, everyone
over the speed limit. I manage to elude the white rectangle suddenly skittering into my lane, but I see the black
tire tracks across its blank face. The man behind in a Nissan truck hooks and drags it, doesn't know a quivering
mass hangs from his undercarriage. At the first stoplight
off the bridge, he pulls up, and I motion roll-down-your-
window. 'You're dragging something,' I shout. 'Thank

you,' he shouts back, waves his citizen-thankful, well-practiced friendly wave, and pulls off, out of the stream. You would be pleased by our civic decency.

The baby at the sunny playground, just now learning to walk, his bottom heavy with diaper, hair wispy and sticking straight out, he's one of five a young woman is watching over, smiling. This little one sees me walking in the lane that borders the playground, and he begins to call, 'Daddy, Daddy,' though the D's are indistinct, more those of a bird-cry in its shrill sweetness. No, I am not the one so deeply desired, that man is elsewhere, his child mistaken; yet the baby's enthusiasm stirs in me nonetheless. Were you walking with me, you would notice, wouldn't you, the alertness in my eye. Would you brush a leaf from my hair, touch the way to begin (and end)?

TODAY ALONG THIRD, a street I'm getting to like more and more because it's busy—just for that, and it's wide enough to receive good light. Up ahead a dad and his little daughter so small she's shorter than an Alsatian, running and squatting down in random places, it seems to me, where she peers at a patch of the sidewalk by the Chinese restaurant that is constantly under renovation and always just about to open. The dad's examining his DVD movie case. When I walk by, the little girl comes up to me, and as I step past, she reaches up and hugs my left thigh. I brush past, surprised. Her father's equally astonished. 'Nicole! Sorry!' I turn and smile and keep on,

trying to remember the look on the child's face: mischie-
vous round pinkness with flopping brown hair and a
mouth that is already shaping into one that would always
expect the world to love it. The father's deeply tanned
face was full of surprise that his daughter had reached
for a stranger's leg, a man's who was passing by, and also
a pleasure in his admiration that he has a child of spunk,
an extrovert like himself, he with the action movie from
Shlockbuster Alternative Flicks, where Randy always
wears a baseball cap and the place smells nice—his
girlfriend's potpourri—and the wood floors creak, the
full statue of armour by the till at the back glinting in the
muted light.

Almost all faces exhibit more than the people themselves seem to realize: over there, in that woman's cocked
chin, an expectancy. Not to mention the upsweep of hair,
the weight of the haunches. And all of us on the search
for something. It's love for the parade of young mothers
with their stroller buggies and fat babies. Holding open
the door to Beans so all that healthy beauty can enter and
become caffeinated.

I wonder about you again, with or without a cigarette?
Night soon, and all quiet, even the terrible TV calmed,
and the book in hand, the latest you have found, the thing
thought, written, said, shared.

B ECAUSE MY MECHANIC has gone a bit deaf—hearing
aids in both ears—presumably from leaning over

racing motors for thirty years, I make a joke about his not hearing the death rattle in my '82 Honda when I take it to him for repair. 'Bruno,' I say, 'if you can't hear the noise, I'm sure Steve will.' (Steve's his shop partner.) Bruno gives me a funny look, and I immediately realize I've jabbed him. I really didn't intend to, but I'd brought the car to him once before, and he couldn't hear the clatter then, partly because it wasn't as pronounced but mainly because of his deafness. At that time, the bearing in the water pump (which I think is the problem) was rattling intermittently, whereas now it's noisy all the time.

On the other hand, maybe he didn't hear me at all. Maybe that's what his face was saying.

As I walk back home, though, I'm telling myself to be more circumspect with my words. I try to soak up the natural world around me as a way to neutralize both my injury to Bruno and my subsequent self-injury. I smell the rotting berries, I enjoy the early morning acridity of the air, I watch the newly swollen flow of Mosquito Creek. I try not to notice the blue shopping cart dumped in the creek and half hidden now under a mat of fallen leaves that has been swept down—and then I decide this modern strangeness in the creek is art. At least until the bridge I'm standing on begins to shake from the heavy commuter traffic.

When I pick up the car later in the afternoon, Bruno's happy to tell me the problem was the water pump, which is still under warranty, and so it's no cost. As he hands me

the keys, I thank him, almost tell him I didn't mean earlier
to slight him.

But he'd just laugh. He might wonder where he could possibly have carried such a slip of a thought juggled among the carburetors, brakes, breakdowns, grease, hoists and the customers he keeps smiling at all day, perhaps one of them in fact you.

Is that why I want to tell you about these cheerful exchanges, the light in the sky, the leaves on the ground, the wind in my face, all that wakes me up into the living day? I want to ask what kind of car you drive, who your mechanic is (if not Bruno), if you have found a male (mechanic) both trustworthy and respectful, if you return to him every time your car sputters and lurches, when in the middle of traffic you hear a new noise in the motor, and into your mind's eye leaps a man in blue overalls who smiles and wipes his hands on a greasy rag before lifting your hood to peer and listen, attuned, understanding, speaking gently and clearly, without jargon, clearest man in the world.

B y 'the world' I don't mean my family, my friends, my doctor and dentist, Nugent the Vietnamese-Canadian dry cleaner, the dog-walkers who criss-cross all the paths and trails in search of the perfect place to pick up poop, or any of the poor who remain patient and hopeful.

I do mean the warmongers and warriors, the Iranian-Canadian punk who walked into the cinema on Esplanade and shot down a rival, the credit shysters whose silver tongues at first promised a phenomenal rate of return, the fanatics who have gone beyond themselves into calm death, and the research-and-developers who put the stripe in toothpaste.

Oh, I know well this combination of sour disbelief and sunken idealism tinged with primal fierceness now that the world may indeed be ending, because when last have I seen a frog that once leapt away from my path, an agitated blob of quivering gronk, plopping down before leaping on into taller grass, wetter edges—or butterflies filling the air out of the shrubs as if they were blossoms let loose to announce that the Garden of Eden was still near at hand and we would be given dominion over all? I feel this state of consciousness rubbing at the inside of my brain where little else can reach. I could lecture on its dangers, set up a support group for Conscious Curmudgeons. We would meet, not in dingy halls with fake hardwood floors and a picture of the Queen, but in ballrooms large enough to contain the half-dozen of us. No CC group would be larger than six—five grumps being the most another grump could tolerate. We'd take turns, we'd have so much to say. Because so much was wrong. And why hadn't someone asked us before now?

Are you laughing your companionable laugh, the kind you would laugh only with me when we walk together on the street? Do you recognize what your laughter

means: that once, perhaps long ago, you, too, were a
card-carrying member of CC—and did you graduate?
How many steps? How many short, long leaps and/or
sidesteps? What kindness entered your life and enabled
you to overcome (or balance) this abject part of your
character? Was it love, from another, or did it arise just as
mysteriously from within?

So WHAT I WANT above everything—is—well—so
obvious I'm surprised and a little embarrassed to say,
it's my own good body 'drawing on what worlds / we
have, in love,' and I am especially aware of that fondness
for right functioning if I picture myself with you and
when I see the same in those around me: The ease with
which the unshaven, beefy driver jumps down from his
FedEx truck, his stocky legs in baggy shorts perfect
for absorbing shock and stepping forward; the smiling
woman with a transparent hat on her blue-tinged hair,
her long translucent fingers folding her newspaper and
tucking it into a plastic bag, all the while looking far up
the street, so capable are those fingers of acting on their
own; the young father squatting beside the stroller and
holding a bottle in the child's mouth, his only contact
with the sidewalk the merest tips of his shoes; the
office man in the charcoal suit returning from lunch,
preoccupied in the crowd of noontimers and playing his
pocket-pool.

The pleasure, too, when I curl into my duvet and

16   prepare to leave my body a notch behind, crossing
      unaware the border into sleep—as I will cross some day
      the boundary dividing consciousness from the tissue of
      itself—and enter into dreaming where, marvellously, my
      body is waiting for me and sometimes takes me flying. In
      a sitting position with my arms bent in front of me and
      gripping invisible controls, I cruise three feet above the
      landscape, cresting hilltops and swooping into green val-
      leys where shrubs and flowers quiver in a wind I create.

      I have a black-and-white grainy photo of myself
      leaping to catch a Frisbee, both feet almost off the
      ground, hands up. When I meet someone new, I shake his
      hand, giving and taking the weight of flesh. New boots
      tell me they are not my feet, not yet. In winter my head
      is a chimney of heat that I cap with my hat. The relief of
      the armpit in the shower after stinky work. The joy of
      skin, on skin (and whose skin you can imagine). But also
      bending down into the fridge for a carrot and suddenly
      throwing out my back, that message from the muscles—
      until eventually their silence returns, and I can step on
      and off a curb without grimacing.

      I've watched the tall lame woman on Lonsdale gradu-
      ally improve. In the summer she had a brace on her right
      knee, a black wrap-around support with a hole in the
      front to allow maximum leverage, which winked like an
      eye when she walked. She favoured that knee, bending
      down to it with each lunging step, her long bones dipping
      forward and back. Today I see her again, and she's more
      upright than ever, only the slightest of limps, noticeable

only to her and me. Both of us know that someday tenderness may return to haunt her, to hurt her, if into the
knee's system of bone on bone should settle an arthritic
node to make her wince. But for now she's walking well,
so much the way her frame can, the long strides of her
femur pivoting and swinging from the hip socket like a
pendulum, a metronome.

I return to thinking of the body's needs for ... other
bodies, the worlds we have when we have love that we
don't have when we have only ourselves. Was that tall,
formerly lame woman on her own, without a partner?
Why do I think that is so? Some mood about her says she
is alone. Women and men without love look at the world
differently, even if (especially if) they have given up the
search for the ones who will help to complete them—for
completion it is, some extra spirit-molecule that flies into
their being from another so that suddenly, finally, their
inner clamour quiets down at least until the irritations
and anxieties and insecurities and oppressiveness rev up,
and the ancient tussle of autonomy and desire begins.

YOU'RE PUTTING ON YOUR LIPSTICK one autumn
morning when across your mind flashes the idea
of the author, that curiosity. How would it help you to
know more about him beyond what you can intuit from
his voice, his way of seeing, his style? You don't really
want me to get caught up in talk about your role and
his, do you? And can't you guess already enough to be

18 satisfied? Or is there a more fundamental question lurking here, about someone who keeps others at a certain
distance and yet yearns for that distance to be breached?

Both of us are more interested in how the world
presents itself than in how the inner mind coughs and
rattles and burns and stalls. All that endless experience
of self with self that everyone feels—and so much itching
for a canny, subtle, sophisticated, funny, intelligent and
compassionate partner (plus beautiful and sex-friendly/
sex-fierce not to forget that peculiar, personal smell of
almonds—or is it vanilla?).

Sometimes words are devils that can enter me without
my knowing, and suddenly I am speaking. Half of what I
say I mean to say, and the other half is them, their snake-
eating poisonous-envy selves that I can sometimes catch
laughing in their pleasure at my uncontrolled tones.

Nevertheless, call me a November optimist: isn't some
good coming? I hope this penultimate hope at the very
moment when the darkness is seriously in command of
the day, and with ahead—at best—some fringe festival of
light, a minor star not capable of preventing my soon-to-
be grand winter gloom. (And are you thinking, why be so
melancholy?)

So I happen to be walking in the later afternoon, on a
street I've walked before, when I happen to catch through
trees the sight of my city rising beyond its blue harbour.
A never-seen-before foreshortened dimension appears. I
am floating over its bright vast space, its towers lit from
above, reflecting glass reflecting glass back and ablaze in

yellow, cream, red, mauve. The sun lowers itself behind
clouds. Some lights dim down and others flip on, squares
in a wall of squares spelling liveliness nearby.

When the wind comes that blows off last leaves—and
nothing but the harbour ships to stop an ocean airstream
from growing—I see the nearness of my neighbours, the
intervening screen of vividly living land gone; once the
year turns down, the outside carries less along, less uplift
of lushness when a blossom fills the end of every ray
beaming down.

Along the street, wives and children ignite picture
windows and kitchen windows. I walk home to my
own patch. On the way, I imagine more light for all my
neighbours—and also, for him, a better fence, posts with
reflective copper tops—and for this one, a taller bean-
stalk so that next year the chance of climbing will come.

Last wish is for myself, the one who's always up ahead:
in the corner by the cars, under the hydro pole, where the
blackberries leap and curl, let there be more than light.
Warmth as well, and juices well rested and restored and
(soon, before I'm knowing it) ready for flowing, yes, and
let there be tenderness, however fleeting or middling,
seasonal or passing, here, with or without you.

B ECAUSE I KNOW PARKING IS DIFFICULT in Lower
Lonsdale, I never expect my car karma to deliver
an opening on the main street, which is why I'm turning
down Second—and there, under the high-rise that looks

like a rocket-launch support apparatus in its upward gesture, I turn into an empty spot, half noticing a woman in a maroon Mercedes stopped in the oncoming lane, vaguely registering yet another honking horn. When I get out, she calls to me with a warbling English accent: 'Did you fail to see I had my indicator on?'

Would you join with me and laugh cruelly at such pomposity? Let us tell those Brits good riddance once and for all, not to bother us with anything other than their perfectly beautiful prose. We will admire their efforts from a distance, on the page—but up close, here in the tangle of traffic, you tell her, please, that we are no longer willing to be patronized by The Grand Mother, those days thankfully past when our submissiveness was taken in with mother's milk. When we defer now, it will be to the west and the south.

Oh, so you don't mind the accent? You actually know a few very nice British gentlemen? You say my colonial inferiority complex is showing? Well, I can change: Say, do you know that Lonsdale was originally just one long trough to funnel logs down to the ships waiting in the harbour to sail away with their cargo to resourceful (and resource poor) England? Oh, those busy English lords and ladies, how can anyone not admire what they flung from sea to sea, I mean, I'm just jealous that I can't enunciate so well, so purely, with such aplomb and dash, eh?

What should I have said? 'No, as a matter of fact I didn't notice' (the truth). 'Yeah, I did notice, but that's how it is down here in scruffy Lower Lonsdale, and if you don't like it, madam, tough.'

She drives off in a righteous huff. I am her righteous huff-maker today. It feels strangely good to have aroused ire in my fellow citizen. I've won some petty little contest in the consumer race for the most satisfaction overall. Perhaps my usual guilt has not arisen because I have finally exorcised a long-carried rage over an almost identical situation: I'd been waiting for a car to back out in a crowded lot, my turn signal on, when an MGB in the oncoming lane turned in and stole my spot, right from under my blinking indicator. I yelled and honked. And carried that lesson in ill civility until today when I dumped it on my English rose. And still how well I remember that other driver, the way he leapt out of his little convertible and, opening the door for his blonde girlfriend, smirked and strolled away, both of them gleeful and beaming, personifications of youthful triumphant smartass mischief that I was not.

Perhaps you choose not to see how juvenile I can be, how masquerading, how adolescently masculine— instead you admire my flexibility, my ability to douse wrath, my unwillingness to fling a riposte I haven't yet thought of.

'ANGIE, YOU HAVE TO REMEMBER the angle you're holding your stick at is the direction the ball is

going to go,' says the man with the beard in the long over-
coat, swinging his hockey stick and striking a Day-Glo
ball that Angie in her mauve winter jacket can't control.

He doesn't have the clothes for a street game. He's a
Saturday dad. Does he think he should be elsewhere?
Probably part of him does; he gets a little bored with her
childhood, which seems to be taking so long. Does he
want her to accelerate through to some place more like
his own? Till one day he finds a whole past behind him,
them, and how clear: the purpose of children is to teach
adults to cry again.

He becomes nostalgic, recalling her in his sudden
fatherhood, part of the eternal triangle, overwhelmed by
what love can do, tears of craziness and happiness that
she is here at last, has come from so far, has called to him.
Now he's understanding this: We spend our lives walking, working, making the brain go round, enjoying the
day as it begins and ends, as birth means spirit becomes
flesh!

Angie and her dad draw to the side when a car rolls by;
I'm already walking near them on my side of the street.
When they resume, a young man on a bicycle glides
around them. They don't notice him, the way his face is
caught up in a long daytime dream of what might be. He's
not wearing a helmet, but a baseball cap's pushed back
to accommodate a big front wave. Can you tell from his
shabby anorak that he's given up on women, letting them
slip away for now, caught up in avoiding that particular
future, the spokes and wheels beneath him going where

he's been already, to a buddy's, some home not his, his a back entrance with children a noise down the lane, his own childhood immeasurably far and unable to provide succour anymore.

Some men are never far from a woman's fondness. We three on Third—middle, young, old—may not quite be among them today. Isn't it time you showed up?

THE THIN OLD LADY WEARS a long green coat with a thick collar of genuine lustrous fox fur on the cold days that bring everyone out for the weak sun. I'd seen her in summer, and although her garb has changed, her purse has not. It still dangles at the end of a strap, at the level of her knees, a black loaf shape that pulls her over to the left. Teetering when she steps, not quite keeping to one side of the walk, she places her long thin legs wide apart for balance. The way she holds her arms, slightly bent at the elbows, suggests she's about to take flight like some jittery, spindly shorebird.

She's so old it's impossible to see her former beauty, and she cakes on her makeup so thick that her cheeks shine, apples among the white. When we meet on the street, she first glares at me, trying to bring me into focus, then returns my offhand comment about the weather with one of her own, her smile transforming her face, all without altering her slow drifting gait.

Her house, an old green clapboard at the bottom of the slope, stands alone among maples and birches—and far below, on the level of the harbour, the street and the railway tracks where nightly the iron couplings jolt us in our beds. On the night of the big wind, two old birches just beyond her wire-and-post fence cracked and brought each other down. Broken limbs, splintered, smooth and bare, and the city's yellow tape mark this place as one for reflecting on windy storms.

I walk by her house now and then. Sometimes I see her looking out from behind the curtain of the back window. The plastic sheeting on the outside obscures her image, but she's the eternal thin tall shape, still and watching the street. Out her front window she sees tugs, container ships, freighters, the far opposite shore of the harbour, but she looks here, where someone passes on foot, by car, land folk she might know.

Is her life now similar to a future either you or I might find ourselves living someday? Better or worse than imagined or expected?

When she looks at me, she who can barely see, what does she find there, what can it tell her, how much would be revealed? She has not lost the gift of reading what the eyes alone can say; I, on the other hand, belong to a later generation that came to rely too much on the mouth and its word-mongering, and when I look at an eye, it can seem flat, and I am soon forced into watching the mouth, the lips, awash in sound I know too well might be false, so that late at night, I retune and retune my ears, determined to catch as many nuances as thoughts in a day.

And were you with me when we meet her on the

sidewalk, it would be you who discovers her name is Janet, she's 97, and she enjoys cooking pies for the two bachelors across the back lane (two who don't live together, she's quick to clarify), and that her rule to live by is 'I never borrow and I never ask for favours,' though she admits she hates the lonely nights.

D O YOU CARRY A LITTLE SILVER NOTEBOOK that you fill up with jottings, ideas that come to you as you're having coffee or reading your paperback? You look out at the passing crowd and your mind wanders, you remember you should get broccoli for dinner (do you say dinner or supper?). You have phone calls to make, you make a note, then look up from the page and see someone who captures your interest, the way he walks, the slouch of his backpack off his shoulder, that moment just before it slides down onto his arm but which he doesn't seem to notice. What is it about him that arrests your attention, that draws you toward him among the dozens moving along the sidewalk? Have you seen him somewhere before, perhaps here under the red awning at Beans?

He looks a bit pinched, too large a forehead, glasses shiny (can you imagine the persistent greasy fingerprint on the right lens?), bent a bit, a touch of the over-fastidious, not quite as upright as you yourself—and yet what karmic clout wants to be played out here? Are you suddenly afraid your radar beaming out toward him will be picked up? You already instantly know he has the ability to zoom in on others, to pick up on moods to such an extent that he sometimes cannot even distinguish those from his own feelings. Are you ready for such an adventure?

Wouldn't it just be easier to put your head down, pick up the coffee and the book, and shield yourself from—what is it?—his longing, not quite for you but for the world that seems to be just beyond his hands. Or perhaps it's just as simple as lust, a chemical reaction that presupposes on the one hand something akin to a long cosmic connection going back through many lives and, on the other hand, some other equally fantastic design or explanation. You've felt it before, of course, men wanting to get tugged out of themselves by a woman like you willing to tug at them, men too proud to admit such a state even to themselves, though he might know himself well enough. Look how easily he enters the coffee lineup, how he smiles at the barista, reads the pasted-up daily horoscope, awaits his americano without agitation.

But you know too well that from a distance any decent man is lovely more or less—you know that if you can admire the body and live with the face then the next barrier is what comes out of his mouth—the words, certainly, but also the tone—and what happens in between you and him: the shared solitudes, the willing- ness to share control. That terrible word. You have already turned against him, in that small second when he raised the coffee cup to his lips, something about his manner, the way his lips reached out, thinking of what he must be like to kiss—and that's enough for now, you say. You pick up your book, smile at your own wisdom in understanding him so well and how he doesn't fit in your life, and you walk away. You remember reading: 'There are few things men find so fascinating as themselves, and nothing more so than the opportunity of remaking themselves in speech, reshaping their past before a pretty audience.'

But does your upright walk and shiny hair prevent you from turning just once to see him? Is there perhaps less acid in your eye when you watch him holding his cup in both hands under the red awning, staring ahead into some vacant and yet no doubt over-populated space?

PERHAPS AFTER ALL WE COULD MEET sometime for coffee. Would you notice that I was talking too much when we sat down and broke open our muffins? I'd be filling the quiet spots into which my awkwardness would flow, unable to manage without words, speaking to show that I was there—a Kilroy moment—acknowledging that you had broken 'through the typical male's self-absorption in the life taking place deep within himself,' that you were the female 'arousing interest in herself, deploying her lures, spreading her bait ... and that other indefinable something which makes the male butterfly struggle dozens of kilometres to mate with the indolent female.' The joys of exhausted butterflies might be mine if you *were* picking up my pheromones, but such

28 gamesmanship (sorry: gameswomanship, gamespersonship, gamesbutterflyship) belongs to the casual young.

We'd meet at Beans, of course, opposite the weekend
stalls for honey and pottery and pies calling out to those
ambling toward Lonsdale Quay in their colourful clothes,
men oozing confidence or just the opposite, though the
stance is often the same, checking their zippers as an
afterthought, women chatting about the shops, younger
men hitching up their drooping jeans, younger women
pulling down their tops at the waist. We could each
provide an anecdote from the week, and if we successfully established a comfortable atmosphere, we could
move onto a moment from the past, not the deep past, not
the childhood trove we live out of for all our years after,
but one from, say, a half decade back, when we were still
who we are now, a moment rising naturally from what
one of us had said. Would this be a painless way to move
along?

Now and then if we felt we were veering toward
revealing too much too soon, we could comment on the
parade of people. Who would you notice? The fortysomething men with their deeply furrowed brows, their
fondled phones? The mother with the crying, pestering
girl-child who howls when she isn't allowed to play
where her older sister dances, on the other side of the red
pipe-barriers that separate patio from street and traffic?
What would you say about them? If we each had to call
the other's attention to one of the passersby, who would
I pick? That sour-faced woman with the dangling white

purse and slanting bosom, her blouse stained by some drink spilled long ago? What would I say: that she seems at ease with her unhappiness here among the jostling strollers? Perhaps I should pick one of the young men or women who stride through the crowd with that strange allure of desire and boredom. Would the conversation disintegrate on the shoals of such treacherous concepts? Back to coffee! Time for a second cup?

I could tell you about that action on Second, though it might upset you. I know you've read a lot, lived a lot, too, and we're both of that age when we're aware of the full range of what can happen to a life, so I'll tell the story as best I can and forgive me if I get carried away.

So I'm on my way to Lonsdale and just up ahead I see a truck angled on the street. The late winter sun shines into my eyes, and I can't see exactly what's going on, something unusual, though I am hardly conscious of it, it's just one of those little moments one remembers, files away, forgets. I sometimes think I should have been a detective, you know? The way the mind catches at the world, a marvellous net.

Anyway, that's not the action. I'm now parallel with the truck, notice it's that deep red and gold of the fire department, when the passenger door opens and a man gets out. He looks like someone from a cop show filmed in Scotland. If you watch certain TV shows, you'll see his cousins: that stocky type, orange hair cropped very short, short black leather jacket, and on his face an expression of rue, not smiling, but grimacing at some unseen unhappiness, and yet not without the distance needed to save himself from any. He's about to do something that he doesn't want to do—that's what he's saying to the world right here. And as I keep walking past, I notice out of the corner of my eye that the driver of the truck is also getting out, though I don't actually see him because my eye is drawn immediately to a patch of whiteness on the pavement: a cat, curled as if asleep, perfectly pure, brilliant whiteness that puts to shame all the blackness and greyness in the world, shining up from that dirty pavement and blinding every passerby with its moment.

Yes, how sad—and also how informative: now we know certain firefighters are even more compassionate than we may have expected—but that's still not the action I want to tell you about. The story goes on. Two days later, I'm walking along the same stretch when I see the cat again, this time in a photo pasted up on the green streetlight pole, and Mimi is looking up into the camera from her pet bed. Along the bottom is a row of phone numbers waiting in their perforated pull-offs, all still there. And across the entire picture, written in deep blue felt marker, someone has carefully printed, *She's Dead*.

That's the action I want to give to you. And here's what it means to me: the writer of that statement knew Mimi was dead, perhaps he—yes, of course it could be she, I know I'm making a gender presumption—he had also seen the cat. Perhaps he had even killed it. But that's unlikely. And, putting the best spin on his message, I would say he decided he couldn't actually take the phone number and call it, couldn't allow himself that kind of close contact with anguish, but, feeling nonetheless the compulsion to deliver his news and feeling the urge inside him of some limited city compassion, he opted for the written message, announcing to everyone and the owner at the same time, distancing himself and yet feeling the good in at least at last providing information.

If you were that pet owner, what would you think the first time you read 'She's Dead'? Think it was a kid's prank? Or a message from the universe. I await your answer. Think about it. Tell me next time.

I SAW YOU ON THE BUS, on the 239 going up Lonsdale while I was walking down. That street is either up or down and never level, and always someone is going the direction I am not. I hadn't thought of you as a bus rider but someone in a sporty foreign car. I wanted to wave to you. I wanted to free you from the reverie of the bus rider who gazes out as the world flows past in the reflected moody face in the window. I wanted you to notice me waving. But you would only wonder mildly, momentarily about who that man was. These wants of mine swoop upon me as your bus accelerates up the hill in a haze of noisy diesel fumes.

Standing there, I realize I want to live in a different time, when I could ask: 'Has anyone told you ... that the rustling of your silk skirt is like the whispering of moss in the forest in June where both happy and unhappy

lovers have kissed? Has anyone told you they would die
for you and that life without you would be pointless and
hopeless?' The age when such words could be said—why
has it passed out of fashion into the realm of the utterly
unsayable?

Or rather why has it passed for me?

Perhaps it wasn't you after all.

I LIKE TO SIT AT THE BACK OF THE BUS because
more seats are empty there, because I can look out
the windows vandals have key-scratched, providing a
multi-layered and perhaps truer view of the city I pass
through, and because interesting people always move to
the rear. I slide onto one of the seats parallel to the windows; and diagonally across the aisle but perpendicular
to me, a large man takes up the space intended for two. I'd
noticed that territoriality on the 239 before: passengers
like to make it clear they don't relish company. On the
239 you can always depend on encountering bags or
briefcases spreading onto an adjacent space. I wonder
what you'd say about such gestures.

By the look of him, I doubt if anyone would want the
flanking seat. Everything about him is either grey or dirty:
his jeans are grimed, and not just from a day's work but
from days of wear. His face, grey and unshaven for four
or five days, has an expression about to blossom into
glowering but which some stronger force keeps under
control. What shines about him peaks from under his

grey cap: a new white cotton bandage held to the side of
his head with white tape. He's had some mishap, it seems,
and I notice now that his sprawl along the seat is not
belligerent so much as awkward and painful. I also notice
the walking stick he holds upright; it rises nearly to the
height of his chin, some gnarled but straight branch of a
golden hardwood smoothed by hands over time.

I have been trying to understand a French sentence
in my travel book, something about revolution said by
André Malraux, and a young thin man across the aisle on
the other parallel seats notices the paperback I am holding up. Reading a book in public is to raise a flag: other
readers are attracted and sometimes feel compelled to
note and often to ask, 'What's the book?' He speaks shyly
at first and then exclaims, 'You don't see books for 85
cents anymore!' And I turn it to look at the cover with its
white and grey sticker in the upper left corner, an emblem
from another time, '1959.' He works for the CBC, so he
says, his curly chocolate locks like a poodle's quivering as
he keeps looking outside for street signs, obviously not a
regular on the route. He talks of Central Asia (the subject
of my book, *Back to Bokhara* by Fitzroy Maclean), Eastern
Europe (deemed racist), Cambodia (the new pre-tourist
paradise, what Thailand used to be) and history. He has
opinions, he is confident, but he isn't sure where he is
at the moment, and he keeps turning while he speaks to
check for street signs, ducking his head down and away
to look out the window so that often I can't hear what he
says, but he seems so distracted that I don't feel I can ask

him to repeat himself, it isn't that kind of conversation, of the person-to-person type: too much chance, noise, others' listening. But it does occur to me that he might know French.

He tackles the sentence but eventually passes the book to the man with the head bandage sitting next to him, who volunteers to read it aloud in French, which they then both do, though not in any synchronized way but as people will when they're battling with a foreign language, blurting out words as their meanings arise; and then the bandaged man translates the whole passage quite quickly into English, his voice vigorous, proud, conveying accomplishment, even triumph, but with no hint of the pedant, noting that we (the others, not him) have been stuck on *maintient*, which I for one thought at first might have been *now*. His pleasure in being helpful seems to give him a new air, one of sitting up straighter. 'Of course I could have just made up the words,' he says—with a little sly maliciousness that is his former glowering self still evident—but when I say his words make sense, he is further pleased.

I'm not afraid to admit to you that I am a little scared of him—the nearness of his pain, the bluster needed to counter any weakness, his yellow horse-teeth, the bluntness of his face-forward look—and I don't want to encourage *too* much talk, whereas with the CBC man there seems to be no barrier to conversation, if only one-sided, and anyway, sitting at the back of the bus,

one must sometimes shout in order to be heard above the
roar of the motor and there has been enough shouting
across the aisle already. I nod and smile, and the man with
the bandage smiles in return, which concludes a quite
satisfying exchange, for me, and I think also for him, of
the kind that can only happen when one hands over a
book to strangers. At the final stop, this large weakened
man mumbles and pushes himself up from the seat, and
someone offers to help but he demurs, and by then most
of us are out the back doors and into the huge openness
of fresh space and sun. The young CBC man, the first to
stand up when the bus pulls to the curb, is still talking, so
perhaps that is why he buttoned up his jacket crookedly.
He the smart, articulate, world-travelling young man,
and the other more the First World War French peasant
wounded in some covert night-time escapade, and me the
book-bearing go-between: we have shared a short ride,
and the unlikelihood of its repetition is neither a sadness
nor even a bewilderment, feelings which no doubt will
arise elsewhere easily enough, and when they find us, I
at least can fortify myself with this memory of pleasant
transit sociability. After all, such cordiality suggests
that life might just be as it seems, bouncing along here
in the sunlight above our collective netherworld of
half-thought, half-wrought creaturely clusterings that
glide beneath us, parallel and out of sight, yet not without
an upward force we cannot deny, try as we might, all of
which of course reminds me again of you.

I T'S SUCH A SIMPLE DAY OUTSIDE: a little rain, a little sun, and along Esplanade I see one woman looking up with bright clear eyes, not looking at anything as far as I can tell, just lifting her happy round face up, her white hair cut close, her smile on the ready to reward not the fellow walkers on the street but rather the sprites of time and place that beckon and tell her she has come through to this fulfilling moment after all.

Down under the awning, a young man rolls his cigarette from Drum tobacco, rolling machine balanced on his knee, empty white tube held in his mouth—and all the while he, too, is looking down the street, not at anyone, not waiting for someone to come along, it's not that kind of look, just a semi-wary glance at the way his life seems to be right now: a little short of cash, a little doubt arising, but the strength in his crouching haunches shows he's as ready as any to make the world he wants.

That boy with the hood over his head, and the young woman with high-heeled flip-flops. Everywhere I look there's strength of soul. I don't have to meet their eyes to know—I can feel these beings stretching up into near-spring light, into the rain that is perhaps a degree warmer than last month. It's not other people they're living for right now—that's for other cities, other places—now they're feeling themselves drift out into the air, into the light, up a little more each day, even planning their return to the mountain trails and to the shore; how long since those days of fresh wind and shushing waves.

I can feel change happening even in me, even in that

mighty moodiness that comes upon me and wants only to be free of itself, all that complicated surging and surfing, twisting and yearning, the ugliness of the near dead thing that wants to be brought out of the spirit's stink and compost and back into flower.

You, I know, would find here earth-warm delight in the gentleness of the old man bending down to his younger woman companion who can't understand what he means when he says, 'Are you tied up for the after-noon?'—her English not able to grasp the idiom, and he, understanding, smiles faintly, fondly, and rephrases, 'Are you busy for the rest of the day?'

S O WHEN I DECIDE TO HAVE MY morning coffee at the Quay, I decide as well not to think about any far-off wars, not to engage certain thoughts that bang and bother me like moths against a night lamp—I want none of it, let my legs leave all behind as I cross St Davids, St Patricks, St Andrews, St Georges. I slay demons at each corner, for each of the saints. I leave corpses under the flowering cherry trees as I murmur about these street signs' missing periods and apostrophes.

At the All Day Café the pretty girl knows I like an americano. She's Mexican, and her crooked teeth don't stop her from genuinely smiling as only the young can, those sweethearts who have so much life ahead they feel immortal (and is that why they walk like gods among us?) even when they know they're not.

'Have you moved recently?' she asks, because she's seen me walking near where she lives, which she calls the ghetto, Second and St Andrew: crack addicts in the alley at night, and when they're not chemically upped, they're drunk and singing.

I drink a thoughtful americano. I've never seen these addicts, perhaps because I'm too early in the morning. Maybe I can't see what I'm not looking for. And I thought no one noticed me, just another guy walking to Lonsdale; why would anyone notice *me*? Where was she looking from, from what apartment window? What might I be doing when I think no one is watching?

On the way home I do notice one man at her corner, and he does indeed look a little rough: he's pushing a rusty bike and wearing a big blue helmet high above his forehead like some Oriental headdress. His face appears weathered from the inside as if he'd been imbibing too hard the night before. I'm staring at him too long, and he's staring back, so I have to speak, and I manage a little dry hello that he acknowledges with an equally arid hi, as if we are both suffering from an affliction of the voice box brought on by living under the sign of the saints with their demands to see and hear only the good in our city.

Oh, you tell me, just enjoy the pink cherry blossoms today! Let them convince me change can be pleasant. I wonder if the addicts might feel this way, wonder if they yowl some nights under these same blossoms and notice their extravagant colour looks fake, like popcorn dipped and strung and waiting for festivities to begin, a celebration marking an end of personal, civic, national, worldly anguish, all gone for a few moments of alchemic bliss.

Four older overweight gents with wrinkled faces—four sample males?—are working on the day's crossword puzzle, presumably because they've heard such an act keeps the brain lively. One has that fierce awkward grin that so often accompanies dentures; another cannot keep his foot from bobbing up and down though otherwise he's as still as a cadaver, apparently not interested in the conversation or the newspaper, only staring out at the harbour but seemingly seeing more or less than its dull grey sheen.

Now I notice others around the food court equally rapt. 'What is there to see that makes them stare for long hours? The constant flux of water holds something that mesmerises *Homo*, though whether it speaks of human origins or of individual destiny is unclear. Moving water has in it a fascination both lulling and imperative.' Perhaps it is simpler: 'The perpetual waltz of light and shadow emptied one of all memories and terror.'

The man with the wrinkled washed-out jeans is sitting alone, not clustered with the others. Like all the men here he looks old enough to be my uncle, but he's probably my age, or why else would he be drinking coffee at ten in the morning when everyone else is at work? It's just that I can't see a man of a certain age without thinking he must be older than me. I can set my clock ahead and back in spring and fall, but I cannot make my inner timepiece recognize that I too have spent substantial time on earth, time that shows in my face and in my hands, in my gait. When he stands up and walks away, I notice the stoop of his back, the indescribable way he leans forward, the manner in which his legs swing slightly out as he steps along. I tell myself that I haven't got to his stage yet. I haven't been made to bend so much. My hair isn't quite so grey. His grimace is not yet mine.

I want to spring up and dance right now. Let rip with a jig because if all goes according to some logical/biological schedule, he'll tip over into his hole before I stumble into mine. Knowing he's ahead of me in that regard, I feel a little better. That's a cheap way to feel, I know, and I hope you forgive my narcissistic pettiness. I promise you that tomorrow I'll be more compassionate. Maybe I'll even talk to him, start up some banal conversation at the coffee stall. Imagine if we became acquaintances or actual friends. How bad I'd feel about how our friendship began: me giving myself airs just because my pants were clean and fresh, closer to new than his. How ashamed I'd be, and what a barrier between us. It would be years before I could admit such a failing, and by then one of us—who knows?—would be dead, and the remaining family would have no reservations about giving away the clothes, or putting up a big barrel in the backyard and setting the pants on fire, all the children in a circle, chanting.

S o three out of five people want to keep their hands empty, free to respond, and I can see why. The man in the one-ton truck parked outside Starbucks is listening to music I can already hear as I approach, and he's rocking back and forth and thumping the steering wheel with open-handed vigour. The identity of the music escapes me—too loud to have a tune—but I see him clearly enough: tight small toque pulled down to his ears (one with a sparkling stone set in the lobe) so that the top of his head seems small and his jaw large and he more of a troglodyte than he surely must be. Beating his wheel, singing along, free of self-censure, his head wagging to the throb, his fingers drumsticks and then his whole palm the rhythm section, he's young enough to feel the blood pleasure, and I see he could be the pushy type, ready to leap out of his cab and wallop me with a tire iron were I to be so foolish as to declaim above the blare of the cacophony that he should turn down his friggin' rap.

Easy to be wrong about people spied from the corner of your eye as you're walking past. I should have noted, for example, that the truck, though big-man-black, was also clean, that his hands were clean, that his ear stud was, well, clean, though I would never want to be so close as to test the veracity of this observation.

But I notice the way that suddenly the volume drops when a young woman approaches and yanks open the heavy passenger door. She's neither feather-strewn nor tattooed nor metal-bitten, but wears sensible shoes and a nylon jacket with a company name of some sort across the back (which I can't read because of the folds), and her effect on our man is considerable: He turns all his attention to her, beaming as if she has brought him a special present and he's a child eager to receive it. His large mouth opens, smiles, his teeth shine. He reaches to touch her, but she needs no help up even though the cab's more than a few feet off the pavement, and she seems indeed to be mounting into his carriage, using a gleaming chrome bar as a footstep. As soon as she's aboard, his hand returns to the controls and he pulls the truck into traffic, gunning its mass powerfully into the smallest opening without causing any slowdown in the flow of vehicles.

I last see them, two tiny heads in the vastness of their conveyance, bouncing down toward the Quay, ready, I bet, to find the quick exit from there and into something even more comfortably real: beer, snacks, TV, stereo, sex, ease of mind, futures like hammers and drill bits everywhere you look, no fretting yet about kids to come if come they may, his swearing saved up for time with his mates and Molson buddies, her tentative giggling queries to her girlfriends best handled over the phone.

Had I the choice I would eavesdrop on her (rather than his) conversation because I assume hers would have more laughter (less guffawing), more intimacy (less posturing), more admitted worry (less bravado).

You on the other hand might prefer a glimpse into his world either to be fascinated or to confirm that you need not be so drawn and/or titillated—that you don't need to spend time there in order to think *I have no interest in that kind of man.*

Later my coat sleeve is plucked by the dirty hand of 43
an urgent beggar trolling the line of the waiting bus
passengers—'I'm hungry, I'm living on the street, help
me'—and he doesn't say please, this black-bearded small
man, a desperate entitlement rising in his voice as if to
say that he has reached this terrible street and now it
is my responsibility to help him—and I don't entirely
disagree, but the only change I have (my handful of coins)
is required by the bus driver, who watches, stern and
beyond irony, and who will offer no altruism if I enter his
business empty-handed. I am next in line, others behind
me, and I wonder why the beggar has singled me out. I say
'sorry' as I step up and leave him with his hands held in a
strangely useless way in front of his unclean coat, and he
bends slightly forward, already looking for some other
source of succour.

Then the moment in IGA when I think I'll find out just
how this smoked salmon is actually smoked, and I knock
on the industrial swing doors of the meat department,
a white room brightly lit, without windows, wheeled
stacks of trays just inside the entrance, some pervasive
refrigerator noise so that the man who comes forward
when he sees me must speak loudly—and I don't hear his
answer to my question because of the vision he presents:
another black-bearded man, this one fat, wearing a
stained green ankle-length apron, and he's holding up
his hands as if they hurt, each one encased in royal blue
plastic gloves, and clustered along these smooth tubular

fingers, tiny incarnadine globes, raspberry seeds of raw flesh.

Later still, sitting in another coffee shop I frequent because the coffee is good and the music not too loud, watching all the hands pass by, those holding other hands, holding leashes, pulled down by plastic bags and purses, pushing wheelchairs and baby strollers and grocery buggies, tugging at the chest strap of the backpack, brushing bangs out of eyes, wiping children's noses, gripping the rails on the bus as it loads and unloads. I wonder how we can manage, not just the mysterious apparatus of will-to-hands, but all that we do and must do before we die—and we have two choices, wouldn't you agree: to ignore our mortality right until the very last minute (and beyond into the very first minute of whatever if anything might begin there even if it's nothing) or adopt a belief system in which the afterlife awaits as does God's love, ready to give us a hand up into his light-saturated pink-cloudy circle. Or do you allow for the choice of being mindful of mortality while living, *sans* God in his clouds, even if too much mindfulness drives one out of one's mind?

In the meantime, I can see from where I am sitting with my americano and watching the street life the man with the baseball cap and sweats I call 'The Gazelle' because of the way he jogs up the sharp slope of the street, his elbows up, his knees high in what seems a nonchalant attempt to fly, so easily does he bounce off the sidewalk, and then down he comes, this time with more loping in

his stride to accentuate even more that utter ease with
gravity (and in his hand I'm surprised to see a collapsible
black umbrella, the first time I've seen him acknowledge
the elements). Two streets over a woman on the seventh
floor of the high-rise, so far away I can see her only as
a figure in the landscape, no facial features at all, and
she is wiping her white kitchen counters, I am able to
discern that movement, that forcing down of the hand to
maintain cleanliness, the sweeping of the arm in circular
motion, her long black hair swinging as she performs
her chore. I wish she would stop and turn to the floor-
to-ceiling window and drop into a mulling time out, rag
in hand, and then come out of that reverie refreshed and
ready to search her neighbourhood beyond the cars and
rooftops and come face to face—though neither of us has
such a thing at this distance—with me, just as between
us, in the back lane, up in the wind, a crow tries to alight
on the top thin branch of a birch, and cannot manage it,
and tries again, his wings flapping back hard, his feet
reaching out and ready to grasp and almost grasping,
and then he has it, ah. Such delicacy in his talons—that
contradiction of strength and sensitivity that you would
almost surely applaud.

S O AFTER A MOVIE DOWNTOWN, imagine you and I are
sipping coffee outside with the smokers. It's raining,
a grey afternoon, and few lights shine from the high-rises,
when a man approaches, talking rapidly, smiling, teeth

46   missing, and opens his long coat. He's confused—or we
     are: is he selling clove cigarettes or a computer? We wave
     him away. Another man flashes plastic under our noses; a
     credit card for sale? No thanks. Young bearded men jerk-
     ily check the ashtrays; one grabs the butts from our table,
     dipping his fingers greedily into the ashes, not hesitating
     to put his lips where strangers have sucked.

     Then a woman with a leg missing below the left knee
     rolls up in a wheelchair, black hair plastered down by
     rain. Her left eye is puckered shut, permanently missing,
     and yet some loveliness clings to her despite the disfig-
     urement. She's about thirty, her voice gravelly, deepened,
     and she wants a loonie, just a loonie, for the bus. You start
     rummaging in your purse, but I refuse. She pushes past
     us, propelling herself with her only foot. A young woman
     two tables down also refuses, and the unhappy woman
     wheels back, bumping our table, crying, genuinely crying,
     her face scrunched in humiliation and outrage. Maybe she
     does need the loonie for the bus after all.

     Do you worry I'm becoming a hard-hearted bastard?
     We watch as the woman rolls toward a girl who digs in
     her bag. I make an unkind joke about naivety. I still must
     pay for underground parking and wonder if I have enough
     cash. All the different levels of economic woes, I mumble
     to you. Yes, we've arranged an afternoon of leisure, but
     we're worried about money, too: we didn't even buy
     lattes, just drank the stuff straight out of the tank.

     Later, back on our side of the harbour, we're leaving
     the Quay when I see the man who often begs there.

He's opposite the entrance, pacing in front of the row
of newspaper boxes, ready to meet me with his gaze.
Balding, unshaven, his clothes rumpled but not too dirty,
his eyes molten, he's always prowling back and forth,
agitated perhaps by the awareness of the awfulness he's
descended into: to beg, to rely on the kindness of others,
to brave scorn, indifference, pity. He asks for spare
change for coffee, though caffeine isn't what he needs, not
with his nerves. On a sunny day a few weeks ago, I gave
him a clutch of coins including toonies, half met his gaze
and felt sanctimonious, embarrassed by his obsequious
gratitude.

Sometimes when I see him, I take a different path
away. Does it offend me that he's still here, that even after
I did my bit for his welfare, my very little bit, he's back,
wanting more? Didn't I already buy his disappearance
with a handful of coins (and is life really so cheap)? I
recall the maimed woman in the wheelchair and hope
she's at least out of the rain; and my hope for her dilutes
the resentment I feel at being reminded that my empathy
today has such earthly limits after all. Does pettiness
draw that stop-now line, or is it perhaps early onset of
compassion fatigue syndrome?

But lately I've taken to giving this man my loose change
when I leave or enter the Quay, usually before or after
coffee. I watch for him, try not to think of him as the
beggar, not *my* beggar, as if I have some proprietary right
just because I give him money. He continues to ask the
same question, speaking it before I am within actual

range of hearing, wanting to establish a claim to my
charity as soon as possible, his voice a plaintive murmur
among the noises of taxis, buses, businessmen, high heels,
cell-phone chatter, children, dogs, gulls: 'Spare change
for coffee today?' From the comfort of the chair at Beans,
I've seen how he chooses those he asks from those he lets
pass by, how he must intuit the psychology of those he
sees before him. Women he rarely approaches, and the
office regulars who come and go have become invisible
to him as he has to them. Actually, he does not approach
anyone (except to take our handed-over change, his
palm open and up and into which we drop our coins,
always slightly wary of him, he who walks back and forth
determinedly, blowing smoke fiercely out his nostrils),
but rather he speaks *toward* the pedestrians in a voice so
quiet it is easy for us to walk by without regarding him,
sometimes with absolutely no twinge of guilt or chagrin,
no matter our views on begging and the homeless. We are
grateful, perhaps without knowing, for this quality of his
voice, for his tact, and for the fact that he is not alarming,
never threatening, for certainly he would not last long on
this corner if he acted even a little bit crazy; if he talked
to himself, turning a wild eye inward to gaze upon those
rousing him to speech, the merchants would complain
and the police would come. We are not frightened, we
half consciously admire his ability to find a good begging
place, particularly on the weekends, to find this niche in
the entrepreneurial scheme, we accept that perhaps our
world here would not be complete without one such as

him, and perhaps we even come to need his presence in
order to understand our own.

He finds his givers most often among young men, some
of whom even stop to take their wallets out of their back
pockets, opening their billfolds in front of him without
worry and then handing him bills. Such generosity
surprises me. I cannot remember myself as a young man
so ready or able to give, though I do know I had even less
to give then than now and fewer unfortunates to give it
to.

When I ask his name, he tells me eagerly—'Daniel'—
ready to offer it as a kind of gift, with the natural energy
one always has when delivering up that part of the self
to anyone, even strangers, perhaps most particularly
to strangers. He says his name without false shyness or
any of the timidity I expect from a beggar who continu-
ally lives exposed amidst the kindness and cruelty of
strangers. Now I am able to look past the too-deeply
tanned, the burnt, the weather-beaten skin, the dreadful
small yellow crooked broken teeth, the nicotine-soaked
fingers, to see someone with a name, and a person comes
into view, not just a homeless nuisance stalking back and
forth. I'm tempted to discover more as the days go by,
where he was born, for example, a simple question that
has a one-word answer because I'm not ready to engage
him in the story of his life (I know he has a story), and I
must remember, too, that now he is Daniel, not someone
placed here for my titillated interest (or irritation),
not a human distraction intended to satisfy any latent

voyeurism, but a man worthy of respect, though perhaps one who needs now to abuse his own self-respect in order to survive. Was there a moment from which he could not fully recover his earlier, happier direction: a loss of job or position, a death, a succumbing to drugs and fantasies, some turn of mind that exerted itself and gave him his current look, one of incomprehension and doubt, always worried that like a child he will be hit? Or was it a slow understanding that grew into a conviction that he was better off begging than working? Wasn't working an option once? Has he reached this point (or beyond): 'Acceptance is what has been placed in the vacuum where for others there is choice'? He seems not to be aware of his animal strength, despite his prowling, so I wonder if some chemical fire is burning and driving him on. I'd like to know how much money he collects in an average day. Does he come over from the city on the Seabus, does he pay for the fare, and if so, does he think of his ticket as a working expense, a kind of overhead, or do the ticket-checkers know him and allow him to come and go, maybe all the while thinking 'there but for the grace of...'?

Next time perhaps I should buy him a coffee, hand it to him before I move on, saying, 'Here, Daniel. Have a nice day.' No, that's not quite right. And what is the etiquette one adopts with the homeless, and how is it different from that used with any stranger? But Daniel is not really a stranger, as familiar as a fellow caffeine addict in Beans one nods to almost imperceptibly in passing or notices and holds back from, though each patron is recognized

as belonging to the morning or afternoon community of
need. When he told me his name, I smiled, ducked my
head down a bit, to acknowledge I had heard him, waved
my hand mildly, gestures that when looked at singularly
seem rather ridiculous, though that's not how Daniel saw
them, I don't think. But of course I cannot say, and even
were I to know much more about him—where he lives,
sleeps, washes, eats, who he spends time with, those he
avoids, when he last thought of his father and mother, his
first day of high school, his most beautiful moment with
a woman, the pet he wishes most to see again, why a certain sweater is best worn on a cloudy day, how he wins
the fight to stay upright, the childhood grin he flashed
around a busy table—even if I knew all these things and
could look inside him as I can sometimes look inside
myself, and assuming he does not become delusional and
seething and thus no longer one of us, I would still not be
able to say with any assurance that I know *Daniel.*

If I talk about him later to you, if you listen to me
when I talk about Daniel, I might say that, no, he is not a
specimen (an example of failed urban policy)—although
perhaps he *is* just that example since there are so few of
his ilk on this side of the harbour while across the watery
divide, in the great city proper, they crowd one another
just to open the doors to the Seabus station in the wan
hope you will smile and flip them change rather than
arrogantly sweep past; there, they emerge out of the sidewalk like emanations, cross-legged with their cups and
caps before them in hopeful supplication; or they wander

dazed and battered deeper into the alleys of the city where needles await them should they need needles to help pass their waiting time; and sometimes at night they at last go prone on the sidewalk rolled up in sleeping bags with yellow milk crates near their toque-covered heads. Over there, citizens must live with their opposite selves waiting for them on their street corner or across from the park or beside the clinic or drugstore, in that city deemed nonetheless one of the most livable in the world. Here, on the other hand, we have only a few now and then who weave their way through the relaxing crowds and expect someone to give them an obeisance and a coin to send them away, in effect paying for their absence. But these insistent, irritating figures are rare; over here, mostly, we have Daniel.

And perhaps Daniel isn't even his real name—though he said it with immediate gusto, even pride, so until this moment I haven't doubted him—but maybe it's his *nom de guerre*, and how clever of him to pick a name that seems ordinary and yet speaks of the lions' den of middle-morning banalities all around, insufferable estrangement from his own struggle. And who dares to say he isn't working: in his manic pacing, his constant assessing, his burning in the air, squinting across the street at us as if we live on the shores of some fabulous land he can neither enter nor even properly discern, only gaining a glimpse now and then when some glittering creature comes through the miasma toward him bearing good will and gifts.

And if on a winter's day I see he is no longer at his

weekend post; if he never tells me again with that buzz-
ing burr in his voice that 'I can drink ten cups of coffee a
day'; if after a time someone new takes up his position,
watched by the security guard on a smoke break by the
loading dock; if and when some such inevitability occurs,
I will wonder: toward what hard, new strangeness has
Daniel gone, to what transformation succumbed? Or perhaps I will imagine him not merely existing in a cramped
downtown subsidized apartment on social assistance
(and I know you would like this part) but risen well
beyond that state and transformed into a clean and
cologne-redolent winner of some cosmic lotto-fortune
and, like a kind despotic king, handing out largesse to
those who pass in long patient rows before his viewing
eye, far from his former isolation.

S O YOU WANT TO BE PURSUED, it's in your XX chro-
mosomes. You want to be made to feel special. Even
at this age? Well, of course, yes, and to ask the question
reveals a lack of understanding and sensitivity verging
on offence; but perhaps for today we can say with Henry
Pulling, 'One's life is more formed, I sometimes think, by
books than by human beings: it is out of books one learns
about love and pain at second hand. Even if we have the
happy chance to fall in love, it is because we have been
conditioned by what we have read....'

So what kind of mysteries do you like? Yes, novels.
Henning Mankell's, with his character's 'tendency to

54 self-criticise, growing gloomy, filled with melancholy'? You laugh! Allow me to reveal my fondness for Inspector Kurt Wallander, bleak-seeing and post-Protestant, an overweight divorced detective reaching an age when only opera soothes, and yet so intuitive, almost mystical, in his ability to solve murders connected to horrific world events now come to rest in his provincial corner of Sweden.

Kurt does indeed pursue the former wife of a dead police officer in Latvia ('Baiba, the woman he cared so much about but never called') across a cold inland sea—and he does so poorly, self-sabotaging, unsure how things stand, stalling, white-lying, sweating, ready to return to the case, to run through information again, obsessively looking for the missing detail that will connect the several scenarios of death and thus lead him to the identity of the killer, which we already know and know as well how high the odds are stacked against our hero/anti-hero/post-anti-hero and his path to that discovery: near misses, false leads, tensions, physical toll, and the killer's sudden awareness of his need to kill Kurt.

So what does he want? Success, of course, and love, connection without a lot of fuss (and distractions from sex, relief from his lurking wariness), peace of mind, holidays in Italy, continual pleasurable awareness that south Sweden in June is a most beautiful world: yellow fields, hills, pine forests, piers and wind—but Kurt the northerner reminds us not to be forgetting squalls and snow, icy fog.

Mostly he wants to get his man, to outwit the devil.
Perhaps such a guy can be forgiven for not putting
forward his most attractive side first. You think?

Or would you prefer Donna Leon's character? Commis-
sario Guido Brunetti, happily married to Paola (with her
dissertation on Henry James and 'finding the obvious in
real life,' her helpful—to Guido—and 'hopeless addiction
to the gutter press'), his Venetian eye for marble and
glass *and* incongruities in a suspect's tale, and always, in
questioning women, a gentleman's manner, delicate but
firm.

Whoever your choice, let him be exotic—and, as a
corollary, let no sudden public corpses under tarps be
arranged near here, no police cars nosing in and parked
dramatically, a squinting RCMP pushing down his heavy
gun belt and scanning those beyond the cordons, his
quick fierce eye contact with the curious, some inarticu-
late accusation driving us away.

I STEP OFF THE SIDEWALK when I near the film set. If
you had been there, I would have stepped off before
you, taking a place on the street nearer the traffic so you
could walk between the parked cars and me, as I act a
human buffer against the speeding deli truck joining
other vehicles now parked along the opposite side of
the street. The brick-and-three-trees area in front of
Champion Karate now sports big black boxes and large
overhead lights, and assorted film paraphernalia fills the

sidewalk. A young woman in a yellow and red traffic vest holds a walkie-talkie at the optimal angle for enunciating clearly into its crackling speaker. One particularly tall blond man and another darker, shorter tattooed one, both dressed in white martial arts wear, stretch and stride about, the obvious good and bad dudes.

Then a man calls to me from the sidewalk. One of those in charge, a clipboard in his hand, he says, all in one breath, 'Do you want to walk over here on the sidewalk, don't be shy, and don't worry about the crew.' He gives this info without once looking at me, his curly black hair and pointed nose manufacturing authority, augmenting his skill in directing people and having them listen to him, confident they will hear a tone that both welcomes and directs. He is already looking for others who, like me, have deferred to the hustling made-for-TV movie happening right here next to Grapes on First, which has pulled in its collapsible ramp used for ease of rolling spirit containers toward trunks of cars. No one resents the intrusion of machines and dozens of men and women; we enjoy the peculiar charm of this inconvenience. On several storefront doors, the notice trumpets: 'The popular Showtime/Showcase TV series 'The L Word' has returned for its 5th season.'

Is this a movie you would like to star in? Well, even if I subvert that L into Love, I bet you'd want something less loud, less louche, less lucent than love can be in its early hours and days, that delicious yet disabling and determined *and* determining debacle of the early infatuation!

We want a script in which you'll shine front and centre,
the heroine, but no longer a young leading lady, we calmly
admit and agree. Would there be room in such an entertainment to play one of the famous grieving mothers? One
stricken, for example, as only Glenn Close can be struck,
her arm sweeping back and down, her voice bellowing
and continuing to bellow non-stop?

Perhaps another script. The one across the back lane
from me. The kind old German lady—no, not her role:
you have decades to go before you sleep—has fallen on
a stone in her garden, the sudden pain continues for
two days, and her husband worries, till eventually one
of the next generation gets wind of it and she goes to
Emergency, her worst fears confirmed: she has broken her
leg. An operation follows, then days of recuperation in
the hospital, sometimes a foul place where patients with
incisions can become infected, her background—born
in Germany—enabling her to see the germs climbing
the bed sheets, microbes, bacteria borne on smells, and
worry before every thought. And so it's at this time, a
breaking point in time, I hear a knock on my door, and it's
my neighbour, speaking to me in his poor, loud English
difficult to understand—he lets his wife do the talking,
I see his unshaven face, his jowls grim, grey, hat pulled
down, his squat enduring body all dressed in brown.

'You help me. My car is stolen and my wife in the
hospital' but he doesn't say it quite so clearly. He's upset,
aggrieved by his own disbelief in the daylight robbery of
his Ford 'on Lonsdale, on the street!' I'd seen his anxiety

when he wanted to open the door before I had even unlocked it. Of course I drive him up to the hospital, and along the way he says more than once 'trouble comes in double.' He says twice that he will pay me. I say no, of course not, I'm your neighbour, I've been to your house, we've had coffee and cake together. We park, and he wants me to come up to the fourth floor and see his wife, too. I think he believes I can cheer her up, return her to her ease of public self.

But now I have errands, and my guilt at leaving him is not strong enough to counter my discomfort at entering into someone else's familial world. We agree to meet back at the car in thirty minutes. I walk to Lonsdale, buy a slice of pizza, eat and hurry back, just in time to see him walking past the locked car—not there waiting, him unwilling to wait—needing to be moving, to affirm the walking she cannot now do. At the car, I yell to stop him from heading down the slope.

We drive home, and as I park in my spot just across the lane from his perfectly trimmed hedge and palm tree, he undoes his seat belt and digs in his trousers, a clumsy, frantic scuffling of clothes and hands, and pulls out a loonie—'for gas!'—which I refuse, not offended by such a paltry amount but touched rather by the resolve of the gesture; and we each insist with some force: his wanting, my resistance—and tears fill his eyes when he accepts my refusal and leaves the car. It has been no doubt an emotional day for him, the worry about his wife draining his energy, so another's kindness flies past all social arrangements and into his sentimental German heart.

So, back to you: Imagine yourself not as the mother here but rather the daughter-in-law of this lovely elderly couple at yet another adjustment in their already change-filled, tumultuous lives—imagine his son/your husband, the hardworking son of immigrants, driving an American car, the son who says he's too busy at work today to take his father to visit his wife in the hospital, the son who tells him to ask a neighbour—and so he comes to my door, where I see that whatever his worries about his wife, his even greater worry is how to live on his own for a period of time so impossibly variable, changing in his mind from hour to hour, from 'she will be home, two days' to something more long term and dire.

Is this all becoming too grim? Yes, we have to cut and trim, shape the story differently, not give you too many moody scenes at the window, better the sunny face-bright moment in the park, or along the boardwalk that joins the wharf running 170 meters into the harbour's waves—and at the very farthest corner of its protective railing, the dark blue metal tubing is mysteriously broken and nothing but a drooping rope keeps you from stepping into the sea, from landing on the back of a harbour seal— 'The Seal Rider'—and then rolling down into PG realms below, bubbles endlessly rising, effortless, from your new body—but just before you dive down, the rating shifts to Adult, you catch a glimpse of a man also at his wharf's end, gazing into the deep, but his hands firmly gripping the solid railing, and as you breathe and leap over the rope, after you leave behind your black shoulder purse on the concrete bench, you see he is running toward you, his right arm stretching out, shouting at you a phrase you cannot hear, you are not in that sphere anymore, but nevertheless you carry his desire for your safety, your future well-being, down with you, and it helps you roll and adjust to your seal-spirit life—while in the face of the man who stops, stays alone up above, we see gasping incredulity and 'a flush of rose ... and the whole thing starts again—'

A T THE CORNER WHERE THE POET LIVES, I look up to his window, hoping some trope will drift onto the wet street for someone like me to find—magic immediacy I transform into my own but he alone flies to the Mediterranean and writes wild powerful poems. What is speaking in him that he hears such sound, that in long sweeping lines accelerating toward extinction, the rain, mountains, rivers and flesh speak up through the soles of one who lives where he was born?

My friends: so few from here, only the poet, and one or two others unique among wanderers. I have imagined myself in that prairie town made eternal by the novelist. A duck hunter, a diligent member of one of the civic clubs, I would discover her novels late. Are we really like this? I'd ask.

Are you, I wonder, a native of here? Someone who
learned to love the shore when it was still heaped with
industrial junk, before it became walkway and park,
when salmon still found streams, when there still were
streams? Are you someone who can spy an old white-
haired woman in the quayside crowds and know her
story, say about her that she worked all her life for other
people, one of the fine old people who greet you with a
fondness that only arises among community? Have you
watched the transformation from town to towers? Have
you paid a sick attention, read the small type of the civic
plans, voted accordingly, protested, signed petitions, felt
the ache that comes when the places of your childhood
are swept away? Have you refined your sense of irony
and distance, affecting a slightly cynical you-can't-fight-
city-hall smile? Have you wept to be such a pawn to the
months and years?

Ah, but then you turn to poetry, to find solace, some
mystery beyond change, mystery even bigger than
change—and you read Rumi because of his irrefutable
truths, you carry Mary Oliver with you now and then—
and then you discover the local poets, or rather you turn
your attention to them because you have always known
they were here, and one day you are mesmerized that the
'mountain sits, dressed in trees, and endlessly clear— /
endlessly clear, and endlessly dressed in trees ...' and thus,
revitalized, consoled, you look up and see old beauty as
new, where 'paradise is so wide, / the junction in the head
so narrow.'

S O WHERE ESPLANADE CROSSES LONSDALE just before the latter runs into the sea, it's a younger you standing near me waiting for the light while the construction noise whirls around us: from above the metal-cutting saw blades biting into their fiercest opposition, the big-drum *bong* when a timber support's knocked loose and falls to a concrete floor in an empty space, that woodpecker hammer chat *whack-whack*, and farther back, a boom box rousing the air with Bob Marley and the Tedium Fighters loud enough to penetrate red and green foam earplugs, some of which have fallen to drift among the windblown, water-swept detritus on the street, where little sports cars leap out with the popping of their clutches, each one a different noise of metal and glass pushing air and propelled by high-grade gas and testosterone.

But you and I don't care because the summer sun is shining on us, the harbour breeze has been cooled by its dip into salt, and we scarcely notice one another until the big double gravel truck guns through the light, shaking the sidewalk, a juddering we're used to, except this time there's an extra sound: a wet splat as the truck's man-high back wheels run over an orange plastic traffic cone, a shriller sudden once-only *yap* that rises above the cacophony—and your younger you looks back at me and smiles, a robust mouth with fine dimples, and says, 'Oops.' You raise your eyebrows above your large black sunglasses and we laugh, civic companions, and then as we step off the sidewalk to cross, I say (as if I am the big truck itself, and why I should adopt *that* persona is one

of those questions), 'Get out of my way,' and we laugh
again, louder, in love with the day, the moment it can
bring, when violence and speed can be endured easily if
the victim is only a man-made fluorescent traffic marker
now quite flattened on the street, split and bent out of
its square foam bottom that ain't gonna direct no one no
more.

How lovely that we can make this small connection,
that we can turn to one another so easily, and we might
think that 'when one feels a compassionate moment in
any civic interaction, when one is the object of compassion and when one recognizes compassion, one recognizes that as a beautiful moment, an authentic moment.'
We are shielded by our sunglasses, never having to make
eye contact, no all-too-naked moment when a swift
glance can disarm us—though such coups can also bring
us into one another, immediate intimacy of a kind—and
I wonder what your eyes would tell me, how much of the
child might still be living there, were I able to look that
far in and back.

Or would I see your eyes, at this earlier age, tinged by
the sadness of losing someone close—a friend, a lover, a
father—an accident on the street, a hospital-bed death at
2:00 in the afternoon, a swift decline—and you not able
to understand why others should live, those so obviously
less worthy, the mouth-breathers and nose-pickers, the
fools who cannot seem to stop talking?

Or would I see the difficulty that comes with being
an ex, for surely you were loved and pursued and caught

64   at last—or does such unhappiness lie farther ahead, much farther beyond this summer moment, in some grey-grim winter encounter when you say to the man who shares your breakfast that he has to leave—and he is unprepared—and who was he? Someone you still half love, or at least care about, not someone about whom it could be said he 'had insisted on treating the whole thing as nothing at all, hoping it would become nothing,' someone (once gone) you can actually see now and then without worry or guilt, who unknowingly took some of your cutlery though you're not going to ask for it back, someone you think you know well enough to take in a movie together until you realize he's forgotten to shield himself from his own drear sentimentality, and now he sobs beside you while the two of you drive away from the theatre, and you can't help shaking your head and thinking once again that like so many men (you allow yourself this cruel generalization) 'he hath ever but slenderly known himself,' and so you probe gently, trying to understand what in the film made him cry all the way home? (And admit it, do you not laugh a bit when you think in these words, that he's like one of the three little pigs, one of the foolish ones eaten up by his own unknowing?)

That's not now, not in this rich sunny now, on this noisy summer street, no, such trouble comes later for you, if ever—and do later circumstances sometimes drive you to become the woman who all her life 'sought to make herself invulnerable, unassailable, beyond reach of the world's judgment. And yet her soul was tortured, exposed'? No, you would not be that woman, for even I can look far enough into the future to see you would not allow yourself to turn from this robust cheer, this 'oops'-happy summer, into the dismal corner of trying to love someone you cannot.

S PRAY-PAINTED IN GREEN LETTERS across a sheet of plywood: *Alex Dose Goats*—and after more than a few steps on the up slope, I still can't figure out what Alex would dose goats *with*? Medicine, wine, oats? Then I realize: Alex *does* goats. Aha! Poor Alex, so nakedly revealed to all who note construction-site notices on Esplanade—but perhaps not so nakedly exposed as the joker himself, who rushed, hesitated, then got it wrong. Perhaps he didn't notice. Perhaps Alex didn't either. I bet you would have understood right away.

Another voice. I'm alone, walking past a very tall younger man with a yellow windbreaker and a baseball cap. He's standing on a street corner's only green patch, with a white and black terrier whose feathery fur comes up around his ears, too fearless and cocky for one his size, which doesn't stop him from eyeing me sideways—as if he wasn't looking! As if I didn't know his designs on my ankle. He jumps toward my pant leg but reaches the end of the line first, his master spitting out, 'Stop it, you ungrateful fool!' Such intimate pseudo-Shakespearian diction for such a little heavy.

Why is language so perilous? Every word reveals its

desire to be something else, wind banging the loose drainpipe against the wall, clunk, clunk, a moroseness muffled by grey rain, the house speaking and saying it wants to be free of gravelly earth and float into air at last. To be past this shape of timber and roof tiles and glass and paint that houses her who returns here daily, the one who comes back and comes back and comes back, throws her shoes off, closes, locks the door, retires, listens, hears inside and out a wind whirling, saying come on—come and discover what arises when language rushes up from not far away, where waves sacrifice themselves on stones to make their sounds, breaking into white and recompos-ing moments later into grey, and above them flags snap at one another and, lower down, fountains mask disagree-ments with their muttering shush, none loud enough to block the snippets of the day:

'... I'm going to say yes, but ...' says one young woman to another, both pear-shaped in tight black jeans, each smoking an extra long white cigarette and walking quickly, urgently going somewhere, but the speaker with less bounce, wanting more to slow and talk, to ferret out the possibilities of what is not yet done

'... they took the fucking fishing boat and he never got it back ...' says the stout man in overalls, blue rubber boots swinging out as he walks, arms also swinging, an unshaven heavy chin, and behind him several skinnier *doppelgängers*, all in checkered flannel

'... but the manifestation itself was real ...' says the tall mid-thirties man, hair an obvious animated pleasure, a winterish scarf, and holding hands with a woman who seems to be recalling a first view of islands and their rare rising out of the Strait

'... she gave me grief ...' says the worker, blue hard hat perched on his straw hair, buckteeth gleaming as he shouts back at another worker, both earth dusty and sliding into already rumbling massive trucks

'... I'm waiting for the blood work ...' says the woman (grey from the part in her hair down) across to a younger yet still middle-aged woman who always sits at the same café table, her yellow hair newly shorn in a way the older woman pounces on loudly, positively ('I like your hair!') before quietening down to her own revelations

'... be careful of the car..!' says the hyper boy, no taller than two feet, expertly mocking his grandfather, who steps around the car and onto the sidewalk and whose visage of slack, bloodless jowls and bushy grey eyebrows the child (I can see it now, already) will come to inhabit

'... I was the first crack in their ego ...' says the man (whose wool cap controls his grey hair) to a similar-appearing man (*sans* cap, *avec* beard) about (I soon learn by slowing my walk) the students he's left behind for good, The Chasm of the Inexcusable Error opening between his knowledge and their bluff and sullen sparkle-spunk

'... shut up, like I'm not in the mood ...' says the stout young father to his wife, pointing across her chest at some vegetable display, all the while holding the portable baby car seat that swings back and forth quite wildly at the end of his right arm, the tiny red-faced child inside about to begin its own comment

'... dat man died in the end—no one told me—I wouldn't have watched it udderwise ...' says the red-faced sensitive, irritated man, waving his hands over his coffee cup, addressing the woman across from him, who smiles and says, 'yes, yes' as if to a child disappointed by a toy, incensed that the thing is other than what he has wished for, that the world is capable of such cruelty

'... B.C. means before Christ, you know ...' says the tall neckless man loudly as he passes by my outdoor table, his black beard and black curls hiding the intensity of his face, unlike the drugged movements of his feet, each barely lifting off the sidewalk, a step not much of an advance on where the previous foot has been pushed toward

'... *you* get the pork chops ...' says the young woman with the curved black horns of hair into her cell phone as she walks past the upscale tattoo shop and glances at the window to check her reflection and sees instead right into the parlour where a body lies on a high table as if etherized.

What you would say to me in this mode remains unknown.

I'M USING THE COVERED WALKWAY that crosses above busy Esplanade when I discover some simpatico city planner has arranged flower beds along each side. An

unidentified scent drifts up, slows my stride. I grab a bit
of green herb in my fingers, rub it, sniff it, move to another
plant, repeat the steps, my mind whirling through memories of aromas. Then from behind me comes a woman's
voice: 'What is it?' She catches up, and we move along
together, almost but not really lingering, still purpose-
ful in our walking. I hear her boot heels knocking on the
walkway. 'Lavender, I think.'

'You made me curious,' she says with a laugh. With
one good look I can take in a person, unless I'm too busy
worrying about what that person is taking in when she's
taking in me. Here's an energetic woman with fine red
lips, brown-tinted sunglasses that don't hide her eyes, a
green scarf and auburn hair catching at the wind. 'I have a
huge sage bush outside my house,' she says, 'and I wonder
why I buy sage fragrance.'

We both laugh because we recognize it's what many
of us often do—look elsewhere for what's near—and we
click a bit, don't we, yes, recognizing irony in our daily
lives; but what does one do next?

Angelina's Cafe is ten steps away, and I'll invite her to a
further, deeper discussion of sage, and then we'll move on
to rain and work as we extemporize, every nuance revealing more of who we are and yet withholding, too. But of
course to extend such an invitation would perhaps make
her suspicious, though she looks relaxed and knowing,
generous, and I could count on her to handle talk, yes, a
sophisticate but not one to mock a man's nerves or his
half-naked need, its sudden ghostly reappearance most

70 surprising to himself, while she, the woman with the melodious voice, has seen such stirrings before, has felt them waft off her shoulders in encounters with strangers along any street, through her ordinary day.

Sometimes one takes dangerous risks, when the soul speaks, announces its presence. But what could we do? We hear our irrevocable lives calling, existences that won't easily be diverted; and now she's descending to Esplanade with its fast cars while I move along, keeping on the level, a hint of lavender nowhere near.

So imagine in the entertainment weekly one of those hopeful, funny 'I saw you' ads: 'We met above Esplanade, we spoke of sweet-scented herbs, we laughed. Have you been wondering lately what might have been? Could it be that with the eye of your heart you saw me in that moment more truly than anyone ever has, more so than even I see myself—and that's why you were comfortable with a stranger who slowed to catch a few fragrances of a vanished afternoon?'

HOW STRANGE THAT I CAN TALK TO HER but not to you. She's there, we chat, then she's gone. But what of you? If I knew where you lived, I could google you, spy on your backyard—but that would be creepy.

And let's hope you don't live on the street I happened upon this morning, with this sign stuck to the front of the car window on the driver's side, a piece of lined paper ripped from a child's school scribbler, the words in green

felt marker, the paper pasted on the glass with yellow dog
shit. The note said:

Listen fuck face if your alarm goes off again at 9 am I'm going to tear open the hood and rip out the horn and smash it through the window. PS you're lucky the tires are still inflated.

Even as I note the missing commas and wonder what male's still sleeping at nine in the morning, I like the PS, not for what it says but for its literary quality, the digression into other matters, slightly (in this case) less severe, the suggestion of softness and hope even amidst the rage. Let's hope nothing like this venom comes your way.

Later that same morning I'm having coffee when a man comes into the café and stands at the front, his right pant leg hooked up on the back of his boot. I can't see his face, but I feel as if I know him, not personally, but something in his stance I recognize, some broad determination, the strength of his posture, clothes all black, the shoulders wide. And you cross my mind, because if you were with him, you would lift his trousers so that the cuff would fall in its proper place outside the boot, you would correct this suggestion of untidiness and error in an otherwise clear impression, and you would do so without fuss, so he wouldn't notice, or notice only that you were attending to him in a loving, partnerly way. He would smile, not for a moment thinking your gesture old-fashioned or sentimental, because it's meant for him and thus endearing and personal, beyond rebuke.

But now he turns, and I see his face in profile: a mid-
30's face, a bit red from the cool air, hair clipped short
to the skull, the nose and lips close together, a dog face,
and all the individuality that I could not discern before
floods in—and I have not even seen his eyes, those founts
of I-ness!—and I see sternness, resoluteness in the sharp
cheeks, the closed-in archness we all seem to exhibit now
as if we're constantly needing to fend off smelly beggars
or ill will, that self-protectiveness that comes perhaps
from a 'hurting of innocence, an end of youth, the start of
a path towards disappointment, bitterness, defeat, anger
with an ungrateful world,' which may very well have
allowed this very man to plaster shit on a car window just
moments before!

Is it wrong or silly of me to imagine that you would
embrace the task of softening this gent (though he is too
young for you), were you his mate? It's not as if I think
of you as merely there for him, but rather that you can
find in yourself so easily the tenderness that allows and
compels you to place your hand on his trouser leg, or later
on his arm, to smile at him without guile or pettiness
or deviousness or even self-interest (if that is possible).
It would be your influence on him that produces the
postscript.

And in me, what would you ameliorate? My nosiness?
You would laugh at me, a gentle reprimand, in your
own way try to draw me back inside some boundary
we had agreed upon without saying so. Walking along
this morning street, your arm in mine, my head up and

watching, now and then the nearness of your body (that
slight pressure, that huge presence) would remind me
that I need not just then imagine so fully or at all what
is happening behind the doors of this or that house,
that I can simply enjoy the walk into the future without
dragging along every second of the present as it turns
into the past. You would teach me slowly, slowly, how
to be free from the weariness of over-stimulation and
puerile, prying, voyeuristic imaginings into other lives.
You would only want me to be free, not just to be with
you (this would be one of your more saintly modes, which
I would learn to appreciate later in our life, when I have
already drawn back from the world not into bitterness
and complacency and self-pity but uprightness earned
and not false), but so you could be with someone totally
free in himself in the half hour it takes for us to reach the
coffee shop, freedom washing over us, and so we arrive
at our americanos as newborns even as we unwind the
scarves from our less than youthful necks.

But secretly I know I could eventually draw you into
the lives on the street, or rather the imagined lives. The
big green house, for instance, the man who looks Slavic,
but I've heard him speak, and he has so little accent
(though his friend Bogdan is Polish and speaks thickly,
Bogdan whom I know from friends who refinished their
wooden floors and he the master at removing centimetres
of old stains and deadwood). What the man does is
unclear—except he is a tradesman: the former U-Haul
truck filled with saws and metal tables, belts of tools,

pieces of iron rod and pipes and hammers the size of my arm, wrenches on the floor under a wheelbarrow. His house has a new roof—he's renovating—and through the upstairs windows I can see the open beams (would you really be interested in beams?—surely you would be pulling me away by now) and the ladders propped against the wall, and also the strong, fine woodwork at the front of the house, some individual talent and expression there in the way the cedar planks slope and meet other cedar planks. The patched-up window below, the colourful front garden borders of large stones and annuals rescued from demolition sites, an act of natural and monetary wisdom, the man himself acknowledges, proud of his resourcefulness in our disposable culture. The Jaguar always parked out front though he never seems to drive it except on Sundays, needing always to run a jumper cord from the house to boost its battery, yet not *just* a symbol of Western decadence (success?) but a good car, those still fine leather seats, the purity of its power when he does drive. The way his sparse blond stick hair falls on his forehead, his clothes always dirty or dusty yet not grimed around the pockets from the in and out of filthy hands (his wife would not allow such a state of dress) but his demeanour born of pride and strength not just in what he's done—buying the old house, fixing it up—but in his ability to live with the unfinished, about which his wife does not chide him.

Ah, you would want to know about her, wouldn't you? What she thought of her own luxuriant black hair, the way it was shiny yet soft, not a helmet of attraction but an unruly yet eye-catching frame for her round face, the pleasant smile when we meet on the street, her pushing the stroller that the older boy stands up on while the younger towheaded girl, with her thin legs in tights always leaping about among the sidewalk bushes when she isn't slumped down whining in the stroller, eyes me cautiously, and all of them speaking softly in some language full of softness, as from the side of their mouths, as if the words were slipping out on their own and making a shu-shu sound in the air. Who would not be interested in this little *mise en scène* of mother-son-daughter?

But you know me well enough to know what comes next! After such apparent harmless speculation about this family, you know I want to spy on them in their unguarded moments, when the children are cranky, when the woman is tired, the man frayed from work, when all the inner resources are insufficient, pride not only not enough but just another task that requires time and attention when most of all each one wants something else: sleep, food, quiet, attention, reassurances, mothering, fathering, especially mothering.

You know that even on our happy walk to the café some part of me is rooting about in the disasters of the family, when lack of money and bad business deals lead the adults to shout, making the children cry, or that time at the back of the house, still unfinished, when the rain entered and then the rats—or so I imagine.

You want to know why I want always to find the hard

moments, the ones which have the dark drama, as if only there is revealed what is otherwise hidden—which you know to be wrong, know that what is on the surface is paid for by what is underneath, that what is seen is also what is true, because you do not believe in a world with so much guile—and maybe you would look at me then, see what I have been unable to hide, and you might feel a little pity then, and feel guilty because pity is not a kindness but a repulsion.

If at that point we came upon the shit-slicked message, you would certainly begin to reconsider what it means to be walking on this street, with me; and how disquieting that I would know nothing of your first steps away, except that perhaps something 'of the sadness of human life came through to me, its indifference to our wishes, even to the wish that calamity should be more colourful than it is.'

So, BELLE DAME DE MYSTÈRE, when I see you next, it's with the man you love, obviously, as if as a couple you 'each found in the other a perpetual assurance that the meaning of life is kind.' You toss your hair, your teeth flash, your eyes shine, you touch his hand, he nibbles from your plate, he with the fringe of white around his head, the rounded top of his head smooth and tight with tanned taut skin, as if he had been away in some sunny clime and has just now returned to you, his heart's core, he with the sloping eyebrows, his virility a comfort to

you both. His pale green silk shirt, open to the second
button to bare his gold chain, moves in the breeze from
the harbour, and around the two of you gathers a languor,
the pleasure and familiarity of the couple happy in both
kitchen and bedroom. He picks up a french fry from his
plate and turns the greasy mess so you can reach it more
easily. That 'the most difficult and desirable thing in a
marriage is managing sometimes to see the other person
as new and unknown' is a fact you have clearly accom-
plished (though I imagine him saying half to himself, 'I
mean, when you're married a while, if you're happy, you
forget a bit who the other person is. It's just like there's a
mirror there all the time'), and then I imagine both of you
recalling the pleasure of how to 'rise ageless / from the
seaweed-scented fishfoam / of our joined bodies,' then,
curling up together with your books, because 'what is
better than reading in the same room or same house with
someone at night?'

But here, now, do you know how flauntingly obvious
you both are, like teenagers, and isn't there something
both sweet and alarming in your apparently unconscious
display of pleasure and desire—and how unconscious
can it be? Perhaps I am mistaken but even the totem pole
where the tourists have been standing in front of cameras
all summer seems to turn ever so slightly away.

And what could have happened, anyway? Had we
bumped into one another in the coffee line, started chatting, agreed to sit together, explored and, well, gone that
next step into companionship and then trust and then

intimacy—but only if we had been pulled together by our genes and stars—would we have managed anything comparable to what emanates from you and your bald lover? We know this: 'We never make anyone happy who does not make us happy.'

The summer air is cooling, the sea breeze bringing something from the west that might be rain or simply the cold breath of the Pacific. I put down my cup and hoist up my backpack. I am not tempted to look your way again. Now I know. So perhaps on the way home I shall need to find more local distractions, as once I found a hundred dollar bill that turned out to be counterfeit—well, perhaps that is not exactly what I mean, not something lying used and crumpled on the ground but rather a fleeting waft of end-of-August. Long grass cut at the end of a lot and turned to hay: This natural ease of change continues while we crowd one another with our glimpses, catching what leaps from a corner of an eye before we turn to gaze nonchalantly ahead where at the moment no one walks but where each of us has city-sauntered, amazed by the array of what we are, and sometimes puzzled and appalled, or aloof, or bending down to examine a stone or leaf or a bit of colour, what's been dropped, what's been tossed our autumnal way.

So, yes, a bit of harvest buoyancy, a fleeting equinoctial sanguinity—until, suddenly, another season also arrives, a nuance of mood, with no forewarning: I feel 'my throat tighten with anguish ... a longing to weep which I could

master as soon as I felt it rise ... glad of it because it proved
that I could still savour the special taste of loneliness.'

I know, I know: *way too much*, you'd say, my sentimental
surging, gushing honestly but gushing all the same,
overpouring here into the autumn the Romantic poet
mastered and that I am drawn back to; and yes, I *do* think
that through tribute all my excesses born of feeling can
be forgiven, because falling in love with the 'close-bosom
friend of the maturing sun' means all sadness I carry can
be dissolved in the moment the season changes, as I will
change, as

> *In a wailful choir the small gnats mourn*
> *Among the river swallows, born aloft*
> *Or sinking as the light lives or dies ...*

B UT BEFORE WE SLIP AWAY into our lives, let's
enter, why not, a parallel world for a while, take the
geographical cure away from the pressures of our home
and native land. We can slide through that door in the
rain, your partner will not even notice you are gone (and
this time out of time is no betrayal of his trust but rather a
possibility of what you might have been had other worlds
developed around you, currents of zeitgeist blown you
this way instead of that, or better still, think of mutual
seduction), so smoothly will we leave and return through
that shaggy dropping fall of water, a plate of pale liquid

glass to which we press our joined hands, and suddenly
we are on the other side of where we were: no more cars,
no more exhaust, we become enlivened like never before,
as if newly young, new in a land until now unseen.

But to arrive there first we must travel through the
dark tunnels of the Italian Alps, great limestone crags
with Slovenian names, and then opening onto the flood
plain, churches high and square, suddenly very different,
and you comment on the light, and you look at me as if I
might after all be someone with whom you could indeed
spend a life. I am vastly flattered and just a little rattled by
your newly winsome eyes, and so I point out the forest,
if forest it is, of poplars planted in rows: my foolish need
to talk when I should have taken your arm, swept you
into my embrace. But the moment passes, and I reassure
myself more such moments must come, for after all, we
are nearing the Adriatic, that great divine sea of pure
romance.

We find our hotel, sign our names, explore briefly the
room, bounce on the large bed, examine the wooden
shutters on the outside of the window, laugh together at
the notion that sun could be so bright and hot as to need
extra *and wooden* shutters to keep us cool. (We cannot
completely forget we have moments before left the
rainforest.) And again we look at each other, our bodies
eyeing one other—and then we remember the beach
outside awaiting our naked feet, run toward it, become
happily grateful we have arrived here in the shoulder
season, for the very carefully marked-off rows of umbrella

stands are empty. We are thankful that we can be lovers
alone (though such lovers are we, we need not notice
others). We select a common stone, one we imagine
was here when Goethe or Shelley passed through—and
then to bed, our trembling in the sheets, your hair a
wave now—when did it grow so long?—and only a little
enough sense of the world we left behind to add melancholy's mild perfume as we lie down together, our legs
touching first, the first nuance of pleasure, the tender lips,
the breaths we share and take together and release and
gasp, even our thoughts in common: 'the future is more in
the unsolid than in the solid,' oh, yes, but the solid, too,
the fully fleshed present—and then the common pillow of
our curved-together sleep where we share no secrets, not
because we have none but because we have no past here.

Our dreams are calm and harmless: 'As if from another
century, it seems,' you say next morning over darkest
coffee, and 'As it should be,' I reply now that we are free of
the weight of our conventional former selves and free to
plunge like half-wild conscious animals into the glories of
Venice; and among the crowds to come we are naturally
safe from all monsters in all futures by the nature of love
itself, its barricade, its flag everyone recognizes intui-
tively whoever flies it, however high or wind-whipped,
safe from the acid rain of deceit and mockery, not one
thread shredding, not one fraying edge evident for some
punk-cynic to point to and whisper behind his hand to
equally sneering companions strutting across St. Mark's
Square that he could see the future for us would soon

enough and inevitably start to unravel—but what indeed does he know of us, we who live so differently from him, he who imagines stupidly that because we are older than his rank youth we live as if there were 'no confluence of river, no / intertwining.'

But first we must take the ferry, the *Eraclea*, we the rubber-necking tourists watching everyone from the corner of our eyes, not ashamed here in Italy to touch one another, to hold each other's hand. We see two old men intently reading their newspapers, a student holding her textbook, and dark-skinned young men who don't bother once to glance at the view as we slide into the harbour full of what you call 'the famous banana boats,' refusing offers, preferring instead to walk and walk and wander until we are made small by room after room in the Doge's Palace declaring what stability and wealth can produce: high ceilings of carved gold and giant Renaissance canvases. Then outside again where I say with you, like you, 'I stood in Venice, on the 'Bridge of Sighs': / A palace and a prison on each hand,' the latter of which we pass through quickly, because lovers are not meant to be contained in any way, desiring instead the watery streets, the smell of leather, laundry hanging, doors lopsided, the stink of the Mercato di Pesci, the graffiti of *Giovanni comunisti = merda*, till suddenly tired, we hanker for a quiet corner to mull a bit—but no such corner can be found. Our pizza is doughy, and hardly have we finished our espresso when the paper tablecloth is yanked away and prepared for a group of overdressed ladies with American accents. We

laugh at them and at ourselves, foolishly in love with time
itself, time on our side for now, thinking we are immor-
tals travelling into the heart of the ancient hot world.
Thus, self-irony on our lips, we take our own photograph
on the Rialto, but then, travelling up the Grand Canal,
we slip back to awe that such old beauty has been here all
along, these houses that can hardly be called houses, and
we imagine that once one of us lived here, we spar about
who, and I concede it would be you. I am too much born
of the northern slope, and you agree, laughing again at my
willingness to please.

We are glad to discover quite by accident the Dali
museum with its T-shirt: 'Life is too short not to be
noticed'—and then wandering again, giving up five
Euros for a drug addiction program—and you quietly ask
me what was it the man saw in us that allowed him to
pinpoint us in such a large crowd. I say, 'We have a new
cosmopolitan look,' but secretly I know he saw more.

Then you walk a bit ahead of me, remembering to be
independent as if you need to remind yourself you can
enjoy this excursion without me. I catch up to you at the
stalls along the harbour, notice the sharp red stripe up the
pants of the *carabiniere*, the way it sizzles in the crowd.
You buy a large bright green handbag so flamboyantly
the new you. We run to catch the ferry back, find our
seats and marvel simultaneously at the way the colour
of the lagoon changes as the sun shifts, from dark blue to
lighter, to green, to dark again, and once in a little wave,
do we not glimpse what seems to be a hollow, a tiny

house we might enter if immediately we throw ourselves overboard, sink down into the ancient water to live enchanted, gladly forfeiting the future with its decline and regret. But the moment is lost, and we arrive back at the hotel to drink lemon-grappa, powerfully strong. We toast to further sweetness, and future hope, reluctant to sleep now because we know we will not dream, Venice itself is the dream from which we will awake, and when we awake next we will be back among the condominium towers, back where each of us will be the way we are, the way we have been: you, delicate and dedicated and happy to be among your friends with your man, your great friend, the hubbub of the plans, the shared meals, the comfort of your future always spiralling out in front of you, the pleasure of its days and nights.

NOW YOU'RE ON THE PIER AGAIN, alone again, wind in your hair again, and suddenly you're falling into the deep, into the water where there is no hope and you will undoubtedly become a wraith, death your nearest moment.

Then I'm there, me with the power to haul you out, by the hair, by the water-waving hair, and I grab your wrist too, pale as a bundle of cigarettes, and pull you free of the sucking water, scraping you along the cement abutment, and just as I feel I have you back in the land of the living, I am overcome with my own weakness, which speaks in me with this voice: *You must never look at her again, you*

must never see her face again, now that she is alive again, you have
brought her back to life, but it is not for a life with you.

Should I just let you slip down into the water, an understandable weakening of my own wrists and resolve?

No, I bring you up like a wet seal, your heavy brown coat sloshing around me like fins, the harbour water spilling from your pockets, your eyes still closed, your face grey with lack of oxygen.

I bend down to give you the breath of life, but just as my lips descend, that voice starts: *You must never look at her again, leave now and she will live, but look back once and she will die.* I am compelled to obey, to step back from this wet mess on the concrete, and each time I step back further you stir, and now you are sitting up, propped up by your two arms, and coughing, hacking up sea water, vomiting. I turn away and run for the land. If I look back, I know you will topple once again into the water, this time forever.

I hold my head between my hands as I run. I will not turn around. I will not glance back.

A MAN, A WOMAN AND A YOUNG GIRL are sitting at a table at Beans, outside because their Irish setter cannot enter the café. The woman is dark-haired and pretty, and connected to the other three around the table the way the man is not: he's detached, held to his other life by a tendril of end-of-week exhaustion that runs elsewhere and away from this grouping, the parentheses

running down from his nose to surround his mouth
showing his withdrawal from even these intimate ones,
and he turns to his newspaper, tipping back his head
so his beaky nose and cavernous nostrils are displayed
upward. He seems a man not yet settled into middle age,
his wife too vivacious, his daughter too young—and yet
when they leave and he stands, he stands crooked, his
back not entirely straight, something already bent in him
that he cannot return to its original upright position.
I notice his daughter stays close to him, and the setter
seems to know that its comfort is needed at its master's
knee.

I watch them cross the street. I am astonished—and
not for the first time—how even more individualized we
become as we age: No other man here has his facial lines,
those nostrils, skin slightly yellowish, that nagging back,
the mien of mild sufferance with still a touch of promise
that a day might yet arrive and bring balm for weariness—and how our families are a source of support—nor
is this news; and yet how much stress a family can bring
to bear on its members, though likely his work not his
family is the source of his pain, and perhaps this Saturday
morning outing has allowed his taut nerves to relax a
little, so that some of the tension of the week has at last
begun to flow out of his legs and into the sidewalk and
away into the ground and into the nearby all-absorbing
waters of the harbour.

Later in the same café, on the same day, I am talking

with a friend whose family has recently exploded: Her
mid-life husband running off with another woman—and
then returning—and a deeper, more complex turmoil
developing—and then leaving again—and I cannot
sometimes tell where the hell of our lives ends and begins,
and which is the underworld and where is the light—and
I am reminded during this conversation about the man
with the bad back who sat on these same chairs just
minutes ago, and I am wondering if he too might explode,
if part of the violence in his back is a preparation for a
correction that even he (most especially he) cannot yet
imagine, so tied is he to the idea that he must patiently
work and endure and *not* live the life he dreamt of those
many years before—but now his old buried heart-life, no
longer tolerating this resignation, is about to spring and
straighten out his bones in a new rage for living.

And so time moves over us. When that man is dead,
what he knew, the pain he felt, the reason for his pain,
will have passed, and perhaps only his daughter will
remember something of him, and then she too will
forget—because we are best at forgetting, at turning
away from the great pile of days behind and at looking
ahead, taken by the sight of yet another eye however
momentarily held, some hundreds of signals and stories
passed along that beam, so much information that one
must turn away, unless of course it is the banal and fateful
moment which locks one with another.

It's just me talking now, without you to listen, and

even I'm not listening, as if it's too late in the day, to both talk and listen, as if there's just enough of me to talk, not enough to listen.

Except to overhear in the cafés the word of the day, someone driven into the shops by the November rain with its promise of spring so buried, someone's story as it unfolds half-hidden, to catch what is made known in the trembling hand, the whisper, the cackle, the silent perusal of the crackling daily paper, the shielding (revealing) book, the sideways glance, the return to the pages' dream.

*

NOTES

8   Upton Sinclair, *The Jungle*

9   Louis MacNeice, *Autumn Journal*

15   Allan Briesmaster, 'Body-Door' in *Interstellar*

27   Anaïs Nin, *Under a Glass Bell*

27   Ludmilla Ulitskaya, *Medea and Her Children*, translated from the Russian by Arch Tait

27   Ibid.

31–2   Gyula Krúdy, *The Adventures of Sindbad*, translated from the Hungarian by George Szirtes

39   James Hamilton-Patterson, *Seven-Tenths: The Sea and Its Thresholds*

39   Anaïs Nin, *Under a Glass Bell*

50   Tim Lott, *Rumours of a Hurricane*

53   Graham Greene, *Travels with my Aunt*

53–4   Henning Mankell, *Sidetracked*, translated from the Swedish by Steven T. Murray

54   Henning Mankell, *The Fifth Woman*, translated from the Swedish by Steven T. Murray

55   Donna Leon, *Death at La Fenice*

55   Ibid.

60   D. H. Lawrence, 'The Ship of Death' in *Selected Poems*

61   Russell Thornton, 'Fifteenth and Lonsdale' in *The Human Shore*

61   Russell Thornton, 'Foot of St. Georges Avenue' in *The Human Shore*

63   Pier Giorgio Di Cicco in conversation with Sarah Hampson, *The Globe & Mail*, 13 August 2007

64   Mavis Gallant, *Green Water, Green Sky*

64   William Shakespeare, *King Lear*

64–5   D. H. Lawrence, *Women in Love*

72   Max Egremont, *Second Spring*

76   L. P. Hartley, *The Go-Between*

ACKNOWLEDGEMENTS

I am grateful for the comments of these readers: Robert Adams, Mary Burns, Duncan DeLorenzi, gillian harding-russell, Walter Isaac, Glenda Leznoff, Lorna McCallum, Susan McCaslin, Meg Stainsby, Richard Therrien, Russell Thornton and Calvin Wharton.

Dedicated to those who appear in these pages and who have since changed.

7   6   5   4   3   2   1

Library and Archives Canada Cataloguing in Publication

Zieroth, David, author
    The November optimist / David Zieroth.

ISBN 978-1-55447-127-0 (pbk.)

1. Zieroth, David.   2. Poets, Canadian (English) — 20th century — Biography. I. Title.

PS8599.I47Z53 2013   C811'.54   C2013-904256-3

GASPEREAU PRESS LIMITED ¶ GARY DUNFIELD
& ANDREW STEEVES ¶ PRINTERS & PUBLISHERS
47 CHURCH AVENUE KENTVILLE NS B4N 2M7
Literary Outfitters & Cultural Wilderness Guides